Chuck

Close

Face Book

Abrams Books for Young Readers · New York

Introduction

Chuck Close is one of the most successful and admired artists in the world today. He has had well over a hundred one-person shows, and his paintings hang in museums around the globe. He will tell you that art saved his life—not once but twice. As a kid, he was severely dyslexic; he couldn't read well, never mastered addition and subtraction, was labeled as "dumb." He also wasn't able to play sports because of a neuromuscular condition. But he could draw, and he got support and praise for his talents. Being good at art made him feel good about himself, and he decided at a young age that he would be an artist. The second time art came to his rescue was in the months following what he refers to as "the Event," the collapse of a spinal artery in December 1988 that left him paralyzed from the chest down. His determination to be able to paint again, even if it meant having to "spit the paint onto the canvas," saw him through months of intense and often frustrating rehabilitation.

If you could interview an artist like Chuck Close, what questions would you ask? Would you want to know how he got started? Why he makes the kind of art he does? How he works? You'd probably ask those questions, but once you saw the scope of his work created over many years, you would probably have a few more. Why are his paintings so huge? And why does he paint only faces?

Unlike most artists who paint different subjects—like rivers, farms, cities, boats, flowers, and people—using the same style (such as impressionism or photo-realism) or the same process (such as watercolor or collage), Close varies his style and his process but not his subject. The extraordinary range of processes that Close employs—painting with oils, acrylics, and ink; drawing with graphite and colored pencils; squishing and collaging paper pulp; making prints, including etchings, silkscreens, and woodcuts; taking photographs; and making tapestries—have been used to render just one subject: the face.

Imagine it is a gray winter morning. You and your classmates are invited to Chuck Close's studio. You are all clutching notebooks, pencils, and note cards filled with questions for the artist. Chuck Close, seated in his motorized wheelchair, a wool scarf wrapped around his neck and a large smile across his face, invites you in.

"So . . . you have questions for me?"

How did you become such a great artist?

Whoa! A great artist? I'm not sure about that, but I can tell you how I became an artist. I was severely learning disabled as a kid. When I was growing up in the 1940s and 1950s, nobody knew about dyslexia and many other learning disabilities. I didn't hear the word "dyslexia" until I was an adult. Kids like me were seen as problems. We were called "dumb" and "lazy." We were the ones always looking out the window instead of paying attention in class. I never learned math. I still add and subtract by using the spots on dominos. I don't know the multiplication tables. I also was not athletic. I had neuromuscular problems as a kid. If I ran, I would fall down, so I was not any good at sports. And I had prosopagnosia, which is called "face blindness." I could not remember faces, and I could not memorize names. This meant I could meet the same people over and over and not remember them. So I was in pretty big trouble. As an elementary student, I thought, "This is not going to be good. This is going to be a great problem."

Luckily, I realized that I could draw better than a lot of my classmates. Not startlingly better. Not dramatically better. But better. I had some skill. So I started putting all of my energy into drawing. And if you just keep doing something, you get better at it. I began to feel OK about myself.

I had tremendous support from my parents. They thought being an artist was a great thing to do. And, I have to say, even though I grew up in a poor town, we had several art and music classes every week, from kindergarten through high school. So

"Art really saved my life."

even if I did poorly in math, did poorly in science, or was not able to read very well, there were still subjects that I could feel good about, that I could excel in.

There were teachers and mentors all along the way who believed in me. In grade school I couldn't remember names and dates in history class, so instead I made a ten-foot-long illustrated map of Lewis and Clark's expedition. I put it up on the wall, and the teacher realized that I wasn't goofing off but was, in fact, interested in the material and

gave me extra credit to make up for my poor performance on tests and papers.

Art was what I did to convince others that I was interested in school. It was what I did to feel good about myself.

Two paintings I made when I was about ten years old and studying with a private teacher. (Opposite) *Mount Rainier,* c. 1950, oil on canvas board, 16 x 12 inches, and (left) *Still Life,* c. 1950, oil on canvas board, 16 x 12 inches.

What made you start to draw?

I grew up in a poor town called Everett, in Washington State. I never saw any art in museums or galleries until I was eleven. But we had magazines. At home we got the *Saturday Evening Post* and *Time*. Back then, every *Time* cover was hand-painted. I would look closely at the covers with my grandmother's magnifying glass, trying to figure out how they were made. A lot of the illustrations were made up of lines, and a lot were done with paint or pencil strokes. That's really what made me try to learn how to draw.

April 23, 1945, *Time* magazine cover. Boris Chaliapin, *Harry S. Truman.*

At school they gave us art materials. If you give a kid a brush they are going to paint with it, or if you give them a pencil they're probably going to draw lines with it. I just kept drawing. I drew cars, I drew airplanes, I drew all the things that kids draw.

There used to be something called the Sears, Roebuck catalog. This was before eBay or online shopping. It would come to everyone's house in the mail, and it was the size of a thick phone book. It was the kind of thing you'd have to sit on if you couldn't reach the dinner table at Thanksgiving. In this catalog were all sorts of things you could order, like clothes, tools, toys—anything! When I was five, I saw a set of artist **oil paints*** in the catalog. The set came in a wooden box with a label that said "genuine artist oil paints." I knew I wanted to be a genuine artist, so I nudged my parents over and over and over again until they bought me this box of oil paints. My father also made me an **easel**, so I felt very professional. And that's really how I got started.

* All terms that appear in **bold** type are defined in the Glossary on page 53.

You liked to draw, so did you try cartooning?

Drawing was something that saved me when I was a kid. I did all kinds of drawing. I drew and painted stage sets, and I produced posters for different events. In high school I made illustrations for the school magazine, and I tried **cartooning**. When I was thirteen, I made an animated film, so I decided to apply to the Walt Disney Studios to be an **animator**. Disney had an apprentice system where, for seven years, people were hired to fill in someone else's drawings. But then

I thought, "Why do I want to wait seven years before I can make something I want to make?" So I gave up on the idea of being a cartoonist.

I was known for my **caricatures**. I actually got up on stage during a high school talent show and quickly drew this portrait of a teacher.

Did you go to art school?

First I went to Everett Junior College, a two-year school that had a very good art program. I got into this college only because I lived in the area. I could not have gotten into college otherwise because I never took the courses that college-bound students take, like algebra, geometry, physics, and chemistry.

At Everett I was able to distinguish myself by what I accomplished in my art classes. Then I transferred to the University of Washington, where I was an art major. I worked hard and was lucky to be chosen to attend a summer art program at Yale University. After graduating from college, I was accepted at Yale's School of Fine Arts for graduate school. I spent the next two years studying painting, drawing, printmaking, and art history with many talented artists.

"I always say, if I hadn't gone to Yale, I could have gone to jail."

Why do you only paint faces?

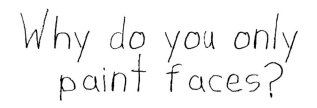

Well, I care more about people than I do about trees or flowers or rocks. And I think everyone knows about faces. Our brain knows how to read faces. It doesn't take much—type a colon and a parenthesis on the computer and it makes a happy face. :) Our brains are just hardwired so we know it's not a dinosaur who is greeting us, it's our friend.

We read a face and we say, "Hmm, I think I have some idea what kind of person this is just by looking at them." They may have laugh lines if they have laughed their whole lives, or they may have furrows in their brow if they have been angry or worried a lot. That's why it is very hard to paint someone your age. I've done it a couple of times, but it's hard because you haven't had enough experiences to alter your face much. It's all pretty smooth—no wrinkles yet. When somebody has lived a relatively active life, whatever happened to them can show on their face.

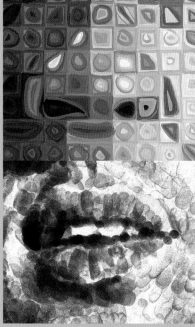

Details from: *Leslie/ Watercolor,* 1972–73 (left eye); *Alex/ Reduction Print,* 1993 (right eye); *Lynda,* 2004 (nose); *Phil/ Fingerprint,* 1980 (mouth). (Opposite) *Lynda,* 2004 (detail). Oil on canvas, 108½ x 84 inches.

"I think a face is a road map of a life."

Why do you make so many self-portraits?

I started making self-portraits somewhat by chance. I was actually working on a huge painting of a female model. I had borrowed camera equipment and decided to use the leftover film to take pictures of me. Through trial and error I got a shot I liked.

I began by placing my portraits inside a rectangle with barely any room to spare. By **cropping** the image tight to the sides and top of the head and high on the shoulders, I found a **composition** that worked because it squeezed out the background and took away any body language.

My first self-portrait, *Big Self-Portrait*, is nine feet high by seven feet wide. The head itself is fifty times life size, so every detail—every hair, eyelash, and pore—is too. I painted it using an **airbrush**, and it took me four months to complete.

I have made over a hundred self-portraits. I often pose rather than have someone else pose for me. When I am trying to figure out a new **technique**, whether I am painting or making a print, I often work on a self-portrait. I guess I know my face pretty well.

Detail of proof sheet for *Big Self-Portrait,* 1968.

Boy, look at me with that cigarette hanging from my mouth. I made this painting more than forty years ago, before people knew how bad smoking is for the body. I am sorry I ever smoked. Do yourselves a favor and don't start smoking. It is not cool.

(Opposite) Standing in my studio next to ***Big Self-Portrait,*** 1968.

The fourteen self-portraits that follow show some of the techniques I have used. Flip the **pages** back and forth to make new combinations. Even though they were made at different **times** using various processes and materials, my face always reappears! ▶

AIRBRUSH INK, PENCIL

OIL PAINT

Do you work from live models or photographs?

Taking photographs and working from them helps me with a problem I have had all my life—prosopagnosia, or face blindness. It is difficult for me to recognize faces, but if I can flatten someone's face, I have a much better sense of what he or she looks like. A photograph does just that: it is a **two-dimensional** image of a **three-dimensional** object. Working from photographs, I make flat things—paintings and prints. That's how I can commit a face to memory.

I use photographs as a tool to organize a composition. I enlarge the photograph and, using a pen and ruler, draw a **grid** over it. The photograph becomes a **maquette**. I then transfer a pencil version of the grid onto the **canvas** or paper, keeping it **proportional**.

A photograph of a face represents a frozen moment in that person's life. The image doesn't gain weight or lose weight, like a live model can over time. It doesn't change from being happy to being sad. You can continue to recycle a photograph over and over. And there may be multiple explorations based on one photograph: paintings on canvas, drawings using different materials, and prints in one or more techniques. I never really abandon a photograph.

A photograph of me with a grid drawn over it to make a maquette, 2001.

When I'm working on these big colorful heads, I first map out a grid on the canvas. The squares of the grid help me figure out where things go. I then place a color in each square. The first color is arbitrary—it's whatever color I feel like laying down. Then I go back and add layers of paint. Different colors sit next to one another; it's something like when a composer writes music. I am making music with paint colors. Just as a composer knows what multiple instruments, each playing different

notes, will sound like when they all play together, I know if you place that blue and that yellow and that green and that orange together, it will create the **shadow** I want or a **highlight** where I need it. And a cluster of those squares, with blobs and squiggles, I have learned, will look like an eye or a nose, when viewed from a distance.

John, 1992. Oil on canvas, 100 x 84 inches. (Above) Painting *John,* 1992, one rectangle at a time.

29

"Painting is the most magical of mediums—all you are doing is rubbing colored dirt over some canvas that is wrapped around wooden bars, using a stick with hairs glued on the end of it."

I don't plan in advance. I make my decisions directly on the canvas, in each rectangle. That's where I figure out what colors to add and what shapes to paint. This process allows me to make problems for myself when I am making my art. Sometimes I choose colors that get me in trouble—perhaps they are too loud or clash with the other colors. Then I have to use my intuition to paint my way out. There is great joy in discovery when making art.

I've experimented with different ways of putting paint on the canvas. This is a color finger painting of my daughter Georgia. I was learning to layer color on top of color, using my finger to apply the oil paint. I was essentially mixing the paint right on the canvas. The individual marks create the whole.

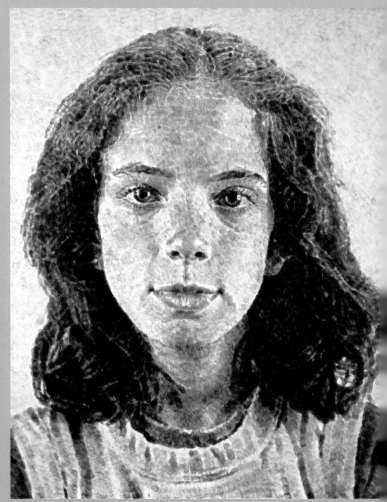

Georgia/Fingerpainting, 1984. Oil on canvas, 48 x 38 inches.

Where did you get the idea to use a grid?

When I was a student, I used to paint big, sloppy pictures.
I could paint one every day. I would put some paint on the canvas and then scrape it off, put more on and scrape it off. I didn't feel it was a particularly good way for me to work. You see, I am a nervous person. I also tend to be lazy and a slob, and I have a short attention span. I didn't want all that to dictate the kind of art I would make—a sloppy mess. So I decided to construct limitations, like using a grid, which would prevent me from making sloppy work.

When you use a grid, you can make big, complicated things out of a lot of little pieces.

What I found was, for a nervous person, having something to do every day was very calming. I used to watch my grandmother, who was also a nervous wreck, knit and crochet and quilt. I saw that it would make her very calm. My grandmother used to crochet, say, stars. She didn't use a pattern, and each star was different. She would make stacks of these stars, and after she had a whole bunch she would crochet them together to make a very big tablecloth. I think watching her make a big, complicated thing out of a lot of little pieces was an important lesson.

How do you make a nose? I don't know. How do you make an eyeball? Not sure. But if you paint a little piece at a time, and you just keep doing it, pretty soon a head emerges. If you like the way it looks, keep going; if you don't, start over.

Detail of *Stanley (Large Version)*, **1980–81**. Oil on canvas, 101 x 84 inches.

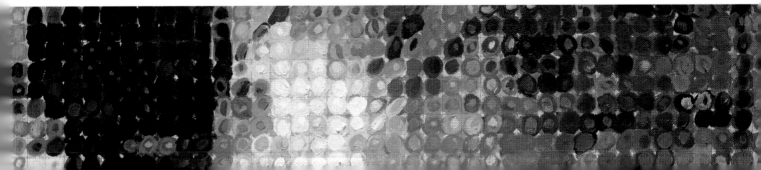

Why are some of your faces in color and others in black and white?

Well, it depends on the photograph I am working from. When I am photographing a **sitter**, I usually take ten or twelve shots in black and white and the same number in color. Sometimes the color image is more interesting; other times it's the black and white that works best.

I wanted to do a portrait of the artist Zhang Huan, who makes paintings using ashes. I photographed him in both color and black and white. The two photographs, taken the same day, are quite similar, so I decided to do two paintings. First, I painted a color portrait with a diagonal grid. Later, I created a second portrait in shades of gray

with a horizontal/vertical grid. The way I made this black and white painting was similar to how Zhang constructs his ash paintings. He uses ash burned in ancient Chinese temples, which is sorted into piles of gray tones and slowly applied to the

canvas. Like me, Zhang builds a painting rather than paints a painting. We both gradually add layers and forms.

I think the shapes stand out more in my black-and-white canvas; you can see all of the "hot dogs" and "doughnuts" that fill the grid. With the full-color portrait, the vibrant paint colors have you under their spell, so you don't notice the structure as much.

(Left) *Zhang Huan I, 2008*. Oil on canvas, 101½ x 84 inches. (Opposite) *Zhang Huan II, 2008–09*. Oil on canvas, 101½ x 84 inches. (Above) The photographic maquettes for both portraits.

Why doesn't anyone in your art smile?

It's true I don't usually show people smiling. If a face expresses some emotion—laughter or anger or sadness—to an extreme, there is only one possible reading of the photo or the painting. But if you present someone in a very neutral, straightforward way, then there is no simple reading of who this person is. You have to look at other clues.

I painted Fanny, my wife's grandmother, using my own fingerprints. I would put my thumb or forefinger into **ink** and press it on the canvas. Look at her face. She was the only member of her family to survive the Holocaust during World War II. She embodied in one person tremendous loss, some rage—she was angry that her entire family had been killed by the Nazis—but

also happiness and optimism. She has a very neutral expression—she's not really smiling or frowning. But I like to think that this portrait shows the evidence of some aspects of her long life.

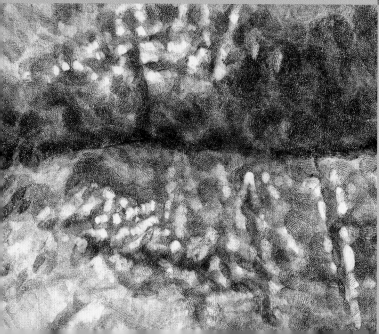

Fanny/Fingerpainting, 1985. Oil-based ink on canvas, 102 x 84 inches. (Left) Detail of *Fanny/Fingerpainting.*

Why are your paintings so big?

Some of my work measures over ten feet tall. When a viewer confronts such a large image, it is hard to see the head as a whole. You experience the portrait almost like a **landscape** that you are traveling over. You might trip over a beard hair or fall into a nostril. The bigger the painting, the longer it takes to walk by, and the harder it is to ignore.

I enjoy watching people try to figure out how far away to stand when they're looking at one of my big heads. They slowly scan it,

and what they're doing is really the same thing that I do when I paint it—they witness the journey that I took to build the image.

The **scale** of my work has made some of my **sitters** uncomfortable. They don't like that every aspect of their face—including the parts they may be sensitive about—is enlarged for all to see. I've noticed that some sitters change their eyeglasses or hairstyles upon completion of a painting. One sitter even shaved his mustache after seeing his finished portrait.

Robert/104,072, 1973–74.
Acrylic on ink with graphite
on canvas, 108 x 84 inches.
(Left) Working on *Robert/
104,072.*

35

Have you ever painted anyone famous?

Well, I photographed Bill Clinton when he was president. At the time, his was probably *the* most recognizable face in the whole world. A few years later I painted his portrait. I always wanted anonymous, every-day people, mostly my friends and fellow artists, as subjects. Then the people I was painting got famous on me. I've actually used making portraits as an opportunity to get to know a person better. If I feel a relationship to an artist's work, I will ask to paint their portrait, even if I do not know them very well. But I must really admire their work.

> **"People lend me their image in an act of tremendous generosity, and with a great deal of guts."**

How did you find your style?

I follow a system to help me make a work of art. Everything, including style, comes out of that system or **process.** "Inspiration" is a word that you hear often. Inspiration is for amateurs. Artists just show up and get to work. Every idea occurs while you are working. If you are sitting around waiting for inspiration, you could sit there forever. I change what I am doing in the studio by changing materials, techniques, scale, size, lines—not by changing my subject matter. I keep myself engaged in the process of making. I force myself to make decisions, and I stick with them. That is how you find your style.

There is no shortcut to anything. It takes a lot of hours to get where you want to go. Through working with materials, I realized that it is important to me that the work is made by hand, slowly, piece by piece. I have tricks up my sleeve and many ways to skin the cat. The key is to just keep moving and trying new things. Out of experience, doors will open.

How do you make your pictures look so real?

Nancy, 1968. Acrylic on canvas, 108⅜ x 82¼ inches.

My first large portraits, like *Nancy*, were **continuous-tone** paintings made with an airbrush. I gave the viewer a lot of visual information—every hair and wrinkle—and they look very "real," whether you are standing right up close or far away. I have also tried to achieve a likeness using the smallest amount of information possible, like my **pulp-paper** portrait, *Phil*. Up close, the grid itself dominates, but as you back away, the face becomes more and more recognizable.

April, 1990–91. Oil on canvas, 100 x 84 inches.

More recent portraits, like *April*, are built from hundreds of miniature paintings. Each is **abstract**, just colored shapes, and I rely on the viewer's eye to assemble the face. I never draw a nose. I never draw a lip. I work methodically inside of the squares or diamonds of the grid, painting shapes. Slowly, over time, a huge likeness of a face emerges through the colorful swarm of squares, ovals, and oblongs. This incremental process allows me to sneak up on the image. I have to trust my gut, which is one reason why I am not bored after forty years of making portraits.

Why do you sometimes use abstract shapes in your "pixelated" pictures?

What you call my "pixelated" pictures are not made by a computer. My hand has touched every inch of the work. But, like **pixelated** computer images, my gridded pictures look like a lot of abstract shapes up close, and more like a face as you back away. Once the marks begin to dissolve, you get a big picture that pushes you away but also draws you in.

I have often used my friend Philip Glass, a composer, as a subject. I have **rendered** his face using many different techniques. I have filled the grid squares with watercolor, scribbled in the squares, and used blobs of ink in each square. Then I began adding shapes and forms rather than just blocks of black and white or color. I discovered that the squares of the grid could become little universes unto themselves. The result is a canvas of mini paintings, which, when viewed from a distance, becomes a unified image.

The building blocks for my paintings are not **symbolic**. They do not stand for anything. I'm a little bit like an architect picking up a brick. You stack the bricks one way and you get a cathedral. You stack the bricks another way and you get a gas station.

(Top) *Phil,* **1977**. Watercolor on paper, 58 x 40 inches. (Bottom) *Phil,* **1980**. Ink and pencil on paper, 29½ x 22¼ inches.

How long does it take you to make a painting?

Well, most of my paintings are quite large, and they can take weeks or months or even years to create. I usually make about three paintings a year. My process of working with a grid allows me to take a big painting and break it down into manageable parts. The different parts of the canvas are then pieced together, day after day, to become the whole. My artwork becomes like a diary of everyday decisions and activities.

At the same time that I am painting one portrait, I may also be taking photographs or working on a print or a **tapestry**. Now I don't weave the tapestries myself, they are woven on special looms in Belgium from hundreds of colored threads, but I take the photographs they are made from and oversee every step of the process.

Creating any artwork—a painting, a drawing, a print, or a pulp-paper piece—means focusing on visual problems that need solving. That takes time.

I have a daily routine. I work three hours in the morning and three hours in the afternoon. I work every day, seven days a week.

" I am disciplined. I work on a regular basis. I certainly don't wait around for inspiration."

Do others help you make your art?

I have assistants who help me with everything except painting. Many of my assistants are artists themselves. They grid off the photographs. They stretch canvases. They pay my bills. They bring in lunch. They drive me where I want to go.

They help me in every way possible, but I work with every mark on the painting itself. Every stroke is mine. Even though I have people around me all the time, I still try to make my time in the studio just about me and the canvas.

Do you ever make paintings on paper?

When I paint, I use a stretched canvas, but I often have a printmaking project going while I am painting. A **print** is similar to a painting because you are mixing and layering shapes and colors. It is the process of transferring ink onto paper using a **plate**

and running it through a **press** or squeezing ink through a screen onto paper. Printmaking creates what is called a **multiple**, because you can print over and over again. Many of my prints are complicated, so I **collaborate** with **master printers**. I often ask them to do things they have never done before. Then the search is on to find solutions to the challenges we come up against.

There are several ways to make a print. For this **woodcut** print of a crazy-looking artist named Lucas Samaras I used a grid of **concentric** circles. Instead of carving one piece of wood, the master printer made the plate like a jigsaw puzzle. Each piece of the puzzle was inked separately then put back together and printed by hand. We did not use a press. The finishing details were added by brushing black ink through a **stencil**. It took over a year to make an **edition** of fifty prints.

Lucas/Woodcut, **1993**. 219-color woodcut with pochoir, 46½ x 36 inches. (Above, left to right) Wood block for *Lucas/Woodcut,* **1993**; the woodcut print in process.

40

Self-Portrait, 1992. Etching, 20½ x 15⅝ inches. (Bottom, left) Making the plate for *Self-Portrait,* 1992.

This **silkscreen** print is based on a painting I made of the sculptor John Chamberlain. It is composed of 126 colors. I created a different stencil for each color on a mesh screen. Ink is pressed through the open areas of the mesh screen with a squeegee. Screen upon screen, color after color, was layered one on top of the other. That's a lot of colors mixing to make new colors! Making any kind of print requires a plan or system, but you

I worked on this **etching** of myself using the same systematic approach I use when I am painting. An etching is a print made with a metal plate. You draw on the plate using sharp tools and then place it in an **acid bath** so that the drawn lines get deeper. The acid actually eats away at the lines! I worked many hours, drawing with different tools to get different types of lines. The magic happens when the plate has been etched in the acid and it is time to ink and print it.

John, 1998. 126-color silkscreen, 64½ x 54½ inches.

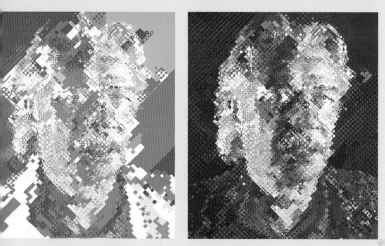

(Left to right) *John*, 1998, State 3. *John*, 1998, State 5.

Phil II, 1982. Handmade gray paper, press dried, 64 x 53½ inches.

also have to be flexible. Starting out, I did not know how many colors the print would need, but we pulled **proofs** as we went, until we got it right.

I love to see all of the states, or stages, of the print hung next to the final work. The states of a print provide a record of the decisions I made. The clues are like Hansel-and-Gretel-style crumbs left along a trail. I want the viewer to pick up the crumbs and slowly figure out the path of my process.

PULP PAPER I started making pulp-paper multiples in 1981. I wanted to explore a new process. One of the familiar faces I often return to is Philip Glass. This portrait was built from blobs of wet ground-up rags dyed white, black, and a range of grays. For a grid we used a plastic grill normally found in ceiling light fixtures, which had squares deep enough to hold the colored pulp. The screen was removed while the pulp was still wet, and I changed the image by pushing on the paper with my hands.

"I am willing to put whatever it takes into making a print."

Squeezing wet pulp into a plastic grill to make *Phil II,* **1982.**

(Below, left) *Jud,* **1982.** Pulp-paper collage on canvas, 96 x 72 inches. (Below, right) Using pulp-paper chips to make *Jud,* **1982.**

My pulp-paper **collages** came about by accident. Squirting pulp into the plastic grills is a messy job, and pulp would often drop on the floor. The paper dried into potato-chip-like discs with irregular shapes and delicate edges. I *had* to figure out a way to use them. I took the dry chips back to my

studio and began arranging and gluing them onto canvas to make collages. *Jud,* my first pulp-paper collage, was made with chips in thirty-six different shades of gray.

Which artists have influenced you?

I have been influenced by many different artists. When my mother took me to the Seattle Art Museum for the first time, I saw this Jackson Pollock drip painting with aluminum paint, tar, gravel, and all that stuff. I was absolutely outraged. I couldn't believe this was considered art. But soon I was dripping paint all over my creations. I had a similar reaction when I saw Andy Warhol's Brillo boxes for the first time. It's that sensation of being shocked, of seeing art that challenges one's preconceived ideas. So I try to go to galleries and see the work of younger artists, looking to relive that sensation of being shocked.

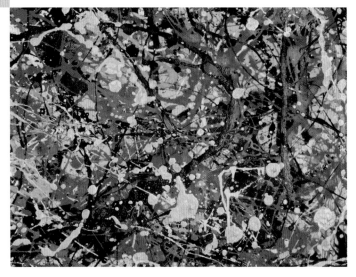

Jackson Pollock, *Number 8, 1949* (detail).

Andy Warhol, *Brillo Soap Pads Box,* 1964.

I feel connected to artists from different cultures and time periods when I understand their process. When I lived in Rome, Italy, I traveled to the city of Ravenna to see the Byzantine **mosaics**. Even though hundreds of years had passed, I felt like I was right there looking over the artist's shoulder. I could see how a corner was chipped off one tile and nudged into another place. Most artwork is a record of the decisions the artist made; you just have to pick up on the clues the artist leaves behind.

Mosaic of Emperor Justinian I, c. 546 CE.

46

Squeezing wet pulp into a plastic grill to make *Phil II,* 1982.

(Below, left) *Jud,* 1982. Pulp-paper collage on canvas, 96 x 72 inches. (Below, right) Using pulp-paper chips to make *Jud,* 1982.

My pulp-paper **collages** came about by accident. Squirting pulp into the plastic grills is a messy job, and pulp would often drop on the floor. The paper dried into potato-chip-like discs with irregular shapes and delicate edges. I *had* to figure out a way to use them. I took the dry chips back to my

studio and began arranging and gluing them onto canvas to make collages. *Jud,* my first pulp-paper collage, was made with chips in thirty-six different shades of gray.

43

When you were paralyzed, were you afraid you wouldn't be able to paint again?

I became paralyzed when a blood vessel collapsed in my spine and cut off the flow of blood to a lot of nerves. I couldn't move anything from my chest down. This is what I refer to as "the Event." For the first few weeks, when I was in intensive care, I just had to focus on surviving. Lying there, unable to move, I started to think about how to get back to work and thought, "Whoa, now what am I going to do? I can't move my hands. I can't move my arms. How am I going to make art?"

I thought about making work that was more **conceptual**, that other people could execute for me. There are many wonderful artists who never make their own work. My good friend Sol Lewitt made wonderful installations that can be constructed by anyone, simply by following his written instructions. But I was going to be very disappointed if I had to do that, because so much of my pleasure comes from pushing the paint around.

I made up my mind in the hospital that I was going to get paint on a canvas again, even if I had to spit it on or paint with a brush in my teeth. My wife, Leslie, prodded the therapists to let me work with the tools of my trade in my therapy. So they took some cardboard and drew a grid on it. They outfitted a brace, normally meant to hold a pencil, with a brush. Leslie found some poster paints—in colors that you would never use in your wildest dreams—and I started to paint again. After months of physical therapy, I

> **"The discipline and determination I learned as a kid overcoming dyslexia helped me through 'the Event.'"**

got enough strength back in my hand and arm to control the brush. Now I paint with a brush strapped to my arm with a Velcro harness. I don't know what I would do without Velcro. I paint using both hands. One hand is sort of floppy and soggy, but using two hands pushing against each other gives me a lot more control.

Did you ever want to give up?

I worked with a physical therapist for eight months following "the Event."

No, there were a number of reasons why I wasn't going to give up. First, I had to support my wife and two young daughters. I couldn't lie there and feel sorry for myself. I had to figure out some way to be able to get back to work and make some money. Pushing myself to achieve something I really wanted was not new. I had to do that as a child to overcome my learning disabilities. The physical challenges of being a quadriplegic were new, but I already had the resolve and stubborness I needed to keep going.

Did the Event change how you work in your studio?

Atop "Big Joe" in 1984.

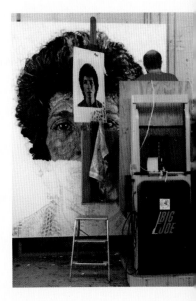

Because I make large paintings, I have always had the challenge of how to reach the top of what I am working on. I used to have a forklift named "Big Joe," to which I attached a platform with a bench for me and a tabletop for my materials. Big Joe could take me up and down, but if I wanted to move left or right, then I had to lower myself to the ground and move Joe over and then go back up again. I would often spend the whole day up in the air. Now my studio has a slot in the floor with motorized tracks so the canvas can go up and down, instead of me. That allows me to move side to side, so I can be wherever I need to be to paint.

Which artists have influenced you?

I have been influenced by many different artists. When my mother took me to the Seattle Art Museum for the first time, I saw this Jackson Pollock drip painting with aluminum paint, tar, gravel, and all that stuff. I was absolutely outraged. I couldn't believe this was considered art. But soon I was dripping paint all over my creations. I had a similar reaction when I saw Andy Warhol's Brillo boxes for the first time. It's that sensation of being shocked, of seeing art that challenges one's preconceived ideas. So I try to go to galleries and see the work of younger artists, looking to relive that sensation of being shocked.

Andy Warhol, *Brillo Soap Pads Box,* 1964.

Jackson Pollock, *Number 8, 1949* (detail).

I feel connected to artists from different cultures and time periods when I understand their process. When I lived in Rome, Italy, I traveled to the city of Ravenna to see the Byzantine **mosaics.** Even though hundreds of years had passed, I felt like I was right there looking over the artist's shoulder. I could see how a corner was chipped off one tile and nudged into another place. Most artwork is a record of the decisions the artist made; you just have to pick up on the clues the artist leaves behind.

Mosaic of Emperor Justinian I, c. 546 CE.

46

Do you have any advice for young artists?

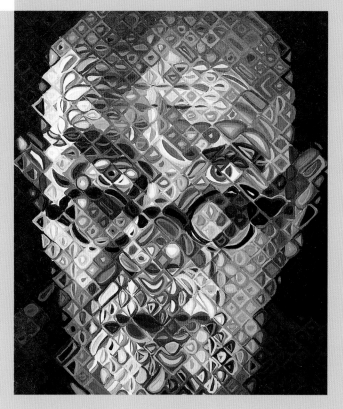

Self-Portrait, 2010. Oil on canvas, 36 x 30 inches.

Being an artist, like anything else, takes time and effort. If you want to be a runner, you go out and run, or if you want to be a basketball player, you've got to shoot hoops. It's the same with art.

Every artist faces the question "What am I going to make?" But *how* an artist chooses to do something is often as important as *what* the artist chooses to do. The subject matter of my work doesn't change—they are all faces—but I am always pushing myself into unknown territory with a new process. You give yourself a challenge and see where it takes you.

Sometimes you have to let go of a project you are working on. I have failures—paintings that just didn't work out. You have to check in and know when you do not like the way the project is going. Maybe I don't like the coloration or the range of marks. It is important to me that I feel good about everything I have finished and put out into the world. Consistency is key; it is important to have the same voice and the same attitude throughout the work you make, even though how or why or what you are doing changes.

In life you can be dealt a winning hand of cards and you can find a way to lose, and you can be dealt a losing hand and find a way to win. True in art and true in life: you pretty much make your own destiny. If you are by nature an optimistic person, which I am, that puts you in a better position to be lucky in life.

"Ease is the enemy of the artist. Go ahead and get yourself into trouble."

A Timeline

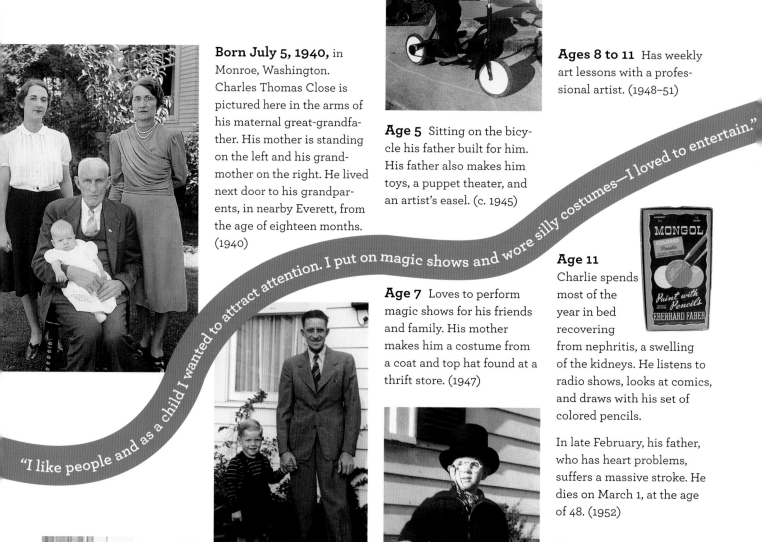

Born July 5, 1940, in Monroe, Washington. Charles Thomas Close is pictured here in the arms of his maternal great-grandfather. His mother is standing on the left and his grandmother on the right. He lived next door to his grandparents, in nearby Everett, from the age of eighteen months. (1940)

Age 5 Sitting on the bicycle his father built for him. His father also makes him toys, a puppet theater, and an artist's easel. (c. 1945)

Ages 8 to 11 Has weekly art lessons with a professional artist. (1948–51)

Age 7 Loves to perform magic shows for his friends and family. His mother makes him a costume from a coat and top hat found at a thrift store. (1947)

Age 11 Charlie spends most of the year in bed recovering from nephritis, a swelling of the kidneys. He listens to radio shows, looks at comics, and draws with his set of colored pencils.

In late February, his father, who has heart problems, suffers a massive stroke. He dies on March 1, at the age of 48. (1952)

Age 12 Enters South Junior High School in Everett. His learning disabilities make it hard for him to do well in his classes, except for art and music. Chuck and fellow art students become charter members of the South Junior Art Club. (1953)

Age 3 "Charlie" standing next to his father, Leslie, a talented craftsman and inventor who can make or fix just about anything (above). His mother, Millie (left), is a gifted pianist. Both parents encourage their son's desire to be an artist. (1943)

"I like people and as a child I wanted to attract attention. I put on magic shows and wore silly costumes—I loved to entertain."

Age 19 Receives an associate of arts degree from Everett Junior College and transfers to the University of Washington, Seattle. (1960)

Chuck Close, *Betsy Ross Revisited*, c. 1961. Mixed mediums on canvas, 86 x 111 inches.

"I was a hick when I first went to New York City. It was the center of the art world and I wanted to be there."

Ages 15 to 17

Attends Everett High School, where he paints sets for plays, does illustrations for the yearbook, and plays the saxophone in both the orchestra and the marching band. He graduates in 1958 (above) still unable to add, subtract, or multiply. (1956–58)

Ages 18 to 19

Chuck enrolls at Everett Junior College as an art major. The art department is excellent and Chuck's two years are very successful. (Below) A 1958 photographic self-portrait. (1958–59)

Age 21 Chuck is selected to attend Yale University Summer School of Music and Art.

Ages 22 to 23

Yale University accepts Chuck into the School of Art and Architecture. He is awarded a bachelor of fine arts degree in 1963 and a master of fine arts degree in 1964, both with highest honors. (Below) As a student, Chuck knows how to attract attention, both with his art and his crazy hats. (1962–63)

(Above) For eight weeks Close takes classes taught by renowned artists in painting, drawing, and printmaking.

On his first trip to New York City, Chuck sees a play on Broadway, hears jazz, and most important, visits museums and galleries. He vows to move back to New York to live and paint.

Chuck enters his large abstract painting *Betsy Ross Revisited* into a juried show at the Seattle Art Museum. It wins third prize but is considered so unpatriotic that it is banned from hanging in the exhibition. (1961)

Age 22 Close graduates from the University of Washington with highest honors. (1962)

Age 24 Awarded a Fulbright scholarship to study in Vienna, Austria, and travels around Europe visiting its cities and museums.

Meets the musician and composer Philip Glass, who becomes a close friend and frequent subject for Chuck. (1964)

Age 27 Chuck and Leslie Rose (above) rent studio space in an old factory building in New York City.

They marry on the 24th of December. (1967)

Age 33 Daughter Georgia Molly Close is born. (1973)

Age 37 Now well established as a painter, Chuck joins Pace Gallery in New York City. (1977)

Age 40 Museums in Minneapolis, St. Louis, Chicago, and New York host Chuck's first major retrospective.

Chuck's mother, Millie, dies of a heart attack on December 30. (1980)

Age 48 THE EVENT Suffering severe chest pain, Chuck leaves a reception at New York City's Gracie Mansion early to get to an emergency room. A collapsed artery in his spine causes paralysis from the chest down. (1988)

"The bigger my paintings are, the longer they take to walk by, and the harder they are to ignore."

Age 29 Chuck's first large-scale painting of a head, *Big Self-Portrait*, sells to the Walker Art Center in Minneapolis for $1,300. (1969)

Age 30 Starts a series of big color heads (including *John*, below) painted using thin layers of red, blue, and yellow paint. He paints one portrait a year. (1970)

Ages 24 to 27 Teaches art at the University of Massachusetts, Amherst. Because of his inability to recognize his students faces, Chuck keeps a notebook with sketches of their work labeled with their names.

He meets his future wife, Leslie Rose, one of his art students. (1964–67)

John, 1971–72. Acrylic on canvas, 100 x 90 inches.

Age 43 Daughter Maggie Sarah Close is born. (1984)

Age 46 Buys a large property in Bridgehampton on Long Island. (Above) The Close family at the beach. (1986)

Age 49 After almost eight months of intensive physical therapy (above), Chuck leaves the rehabilitation hospital. He regains enough strength and control to paint but is confined to a wheelchair and requires daily nursing care.

The first canvas he paints after "the Event" is a small portrait of Alex Katz. (1989)

Alex II, 1989. Oil on canvas, 36 x 30 inches.

Age 51
Close is invited to curate a show at the Museum of Modern Art in New York. *Head On/The Modern Portrait* marks Chuck's reentry into the public art world. (1991)

Age 55
Receives numerous honorary degrees, including a doctorate of fine arts from Yale University. (1996)

Age 57
The Museum of Modern Art organizes a major retrospective of Close's work that travels to Chicago, Washington, D.C., Seattle, and London. (1998)

Chuck installing his 1998 retrospective in New York with MoMA curator Robert Storr. Photograph by Tina Barney.

"I think problem solving is highly overrated. Problem creation is much more interesting."

Moves to his present studio on Bond Street in New York City. He retires his forklift "Big Joe" and installs a slot in the floor and motorized tracks so his canvases can be raised or lowered. (1992)

Age 54
Chuck paints artist Roy Lichtenstein, one of the New York art world's most famous faces. (1994)

Roy II, 1994. Oil on canvas, 102 x 84 inches.

Age 60
Chuck is awarded the National Medal of Arts and honored at the White House. (2000)

Age 61
Big Bird visits Chuck's studio to talk about his portraits. Three episodes are taped to air on *Sesame Street*. (2001)

Age 63
Chuck Close: Process and Collaboration, an exhibition focusing on Chuck's printmaking career is launched in Houston and travels to over a dozen museums across the country. (2003–present)

President Bill Clinton, 2006. Oil on canvas, 108½ x 84 inches.

Age 66
Paints former President Clinton's portrait from a photograph he took a year earlier. This was his first painting of an "instantly recognizable" face. (2006)

Kate, 2007. Jacquard tapestry, 103 x 79 inches.

Working from daguerreotypes (photographic images made using an hundred-and-fifty-year-old process) Close begins a series of oversized portrait tapestries. (2006–present)

Age 71
President Obama appoints Chuck to the President's Committee on the Arts and the Humanities. (2011)

Resources

MUSEUMS

These are some of the many museums you can visit to see real work by Chuck Close! To find the artist's work on a museum's website, click on "collections" and search for "Chuck Close."

Albright-Knox Art Gallery, Buffalo, New York
www.albrightknox.org

Art Gallery of Ontario, Toronto, Canada
www.ago.net

Art Institute of Chicago, Chicago, Illinois
www.artic.edu/aic

The Cleveland Museum of Art, Cleveland, Ohio
www.clevelandart.org

Dallas Museum of Art, Dallas, Texas
www.dallasmuseumofart.org

Solomon R. Guggenheim Muesum, New York, New York
www.guggenheim.org

High Museum of Art, Atlanta, Georgia
www.high.org

The Hirshhorn Museum and Sculpture Garden, Smithsonian Institution, Washington, D.C.
www.hirshhorn.si.edu

Los Angeles County Museum of Art, Los Angeles, California
www.lacma.org

The Metropolitan Museum of Art, New York, New York
www.metmuseum.org

Milwaukee Art Museum, Milwaukee, Wisconsin
www.mam.org

Museum of Contemporary Art, Chicago, Illinois
www.mcachicago.org

Museum of Fine Arts, Boston, Massachusetts
www.mfa.org

Museum of Modern Art, New York, New York
www.moma.org

Museum of Modern Art of Fort Worth, Fort Worth, Texas
www. themodern.org

National Gallery of Australia, Canberra, Australia
artsearch.nga.gov.au

National Gallery of Canada, Ottawa, Canada
www.gallery.ca

National Portrait Gallery, Washington, D.C.
www.npg.si.edu

Nelson-Atkins Museum of Art, Kansas City, Missouri
www.nelson-atkins.org

San Francisco Museum of Modern Art, San Francisco, California
www.sfmoma.org

Seattle Art Museum, Seattle, Washington
www.seattleartmuseum.org

Tate Gallery, London, Great Britain
www.tate.org.uk

Toledo Museum of Art, Toledo, Ohio
www.toledomuseum.org

Virginia Museum of Fine Art, Richmond, Virginia
www.vmfa.state.va.us

Walker Art Center, Minneapolis, Minnesota
www.collections.walkerart.org

Whitney Museum of American Art, New York, New York
whitney.org

BOOKS

Close, Chuck, Dave Hickey, William Bartman, and Joanne Kesten. *The Portraits Speak: Chuck Close in Conversation with 27 of His Subjects.* New York: A.R.T. Press, 1997.

Close, Chuck, Robert Holman, and Lyle Rexer. *Chuck Close: A Couple of Ways of Doing Something.* New York: Aperture, 2006.

Close, Chuck, Robert Storr, Kirk Varnedoe, Deborah Wye, and Glenn D. Lowry. *Chuck Close.* New York: Museum of Modern Art, 2002.

Finch, Christopher. *Chuck Close: Life.* New York: Prestel, 2010.

——. *Chuck Close: Work.* New York: Prestel, 2007.

Friedman, Martin. *Close Reading: Chuck Close and the Artist Portrait.* New York: Harry N. Abrams, 2005.

Grynsztejn, Madeleine, and Siri Engberg. *Chuck Close: Self-Portraits 1967–2005.* San Francisco: San Francisco Museum of Modern Art and Minneapolis: Walker Art Center, 2005.

Sultan, Terrie. *Chuck Close Prints: Process and Collaboration.* New Jersey: Princeton University Press, 2003.

WEBSITES

Chuck Close's gallery
thepacegallery.com

Links to Chuck Close works online
www.artcyclopedia.com/artists/close_chuck.html

Chuck Close Prints: Process and Collaboration
www.chuckclose.coe.uh.edu/

ONLINE VIDEOS

The Artist's Studio: Chuck Close
www.plumtv.com/videos/artists-studio-chuck-close

Chuck Close: Why Portraits?
www.sfmoma.org/explore/multimedia/videos/376

Making pulp-paper prints
www.youtube.com/watch?v=_9R7BzJMxfs

Glossary

Note: The numbers in parentheses refer to the pages where the term appears.

Abstract: Not representing or imitating real life; the opposite of realistic. (37, 38)

Acid bath: A tray of acid (the bath) that is used to etch, or bite, the lines of a metal plate to different depths depending on how long the metal stays in the bath. (41)

Airbrush: A small air-operated tool that sprays ink, dye, or paint onto a surface such as paper or canvas. (12, 14, 16, 37)

Animator: An artist who creates multiple images that give the illusion of movement. Animators often work in film, television, and video games and on web-based imagery. (9)

Canvas: A heavy-duty woven fabric used by artists as a painting surface, typically stretched across a wooden frame. (4, 28, 29, 30, 31, 32, 34, 38, 39, 40, 43, 44, 45)

Caricature: A portrait that exaggerates the features of a person or thing. (9)

Cartoons: Single-panel drawings that are usually humorous. (9)

Continuous tone: Images that have a virtually unlimited range of color or shades of grays. Photographs are continuous tone. (37)

Collaborate: When two or more people work together to achieve a common goal. (40)

Collage: From the French verb *coller* (to stick or paste); refers to the process of combining and attaching paper and other objects to a surface using glue. (4, 43)

Composition: The way things are arranged in a work of art. (12, 28)

Concentric: When two or more shapes share the same center point. A target has concentric circles. (40)

Conceptual: When the idea is more important than the actual work of art. (44)

Cropping: A technique used to reframe and squeeze an image in tighter. Chuck Close crops his portraits. (12)

Easel: An upright stand used for holding a canvas. (8)

Edition: The number of prints made from one plate. (40)

Etching: An old method of printmaking in which the artist uses acid to cut into the unprotected parts of a metal surface to create a design. The surface is then inked and printed. Intaglio and engraving are two types of etchings. (4, 18, 41)

Grid: A framework of crisscrossed parallel lines that creates an organized series of equal-sized shapes. Chuck Close uses the grid as the basis of his work. (28, 29, 31, 32, 37, 38, 40, 42, 44)

Highlight: An area in a drawing, painting, or photograph that is much lighter. (29)

Ink: A thick paste that contains color that is used for printmaking. Ink can be rolled on (woodcuts), squeezed (silkscreen), or applied with a rag (etchings). (4, 34, 38, 40, 41)

Landscape: The depiction of natural scenery, such as mountains, valleys, trees, rivers, and forests. (35)

Maquette: French word for "scale model." Used to visualize and test shapes and ideas before making the final work of art. (28, 32)

Master printer: A skilled person who has the job of working with other artists to make prints in a print shop. (40)

Mosaics: The art of creating images by piecing together small bits of colored glass, stone, or ceramics. (46)

Multiple: Making more than one image. When making prints, printmakers pull many images, which collectively make up an edition. (40, 42)

Oil paint: A type of slow-drying paint that consists of particles of pigment mixed with linseed oil. (8, 15, 17, 21, 25, 27, 30)

Pixelated: Having a visible pattern of dots that, when looked at from a distance, create an image. (38)

Plate: The surface in printmaking that carries the image to be printed. The image on the surface can be raised (woodcut) or carved (etching). (40, 41)

Pochoir: The French word for stencil. A technique for hand-coloring a print using stencils. (40)

Press: A machine with a heavy roller that transfers inked lettering or images onto another surface, like paper. (40)

Print: A mark or impression made on a surface by using pressure. In printmaking, it is the finished image that results from the transfer of ink onto paper using a plate. (4, 12, 28, 39, 40, 41, 42)

Process: A series of actions or steps taken to achieve a result. (4, 13, 36, 37, 39, 40, 42, 46, 47)

Proof: In printmaking, a test print that is pulled so that the artist can see what work still needs to be done to the plate. (42)

Proportional: Describing the relative size of things; something is proportional if it is always larger or smaller by the same amount. (28)

Pulp paper: A material made out of wet wood fibers that are broken down to be used for papermaking. (20, 37, 39, 42–43)

Rendered: Reproduced or represented using art materials. (38)

Scale: The size of an object in relation to another object. (35, 36)

Shadow: A dark spot in an area of a painting or sculpture where light cannot reach because an object is in the way. (29)

Silkscreen: A stencil method of printmaking. A design is made on a screen of silk, and ink is pushed through the open areas using a squeegee, a tool with a rubber-edged blade. (4, 41–42)

Sitter: A person who poses or models for an artist. (32, 35)

Stencil: A thin sheet of material, such as paper, plastic, or metal, with letters or a design cut from it. (40, 41)

Symbolic: A visible object or design that represents something invisible, like an idea. (38)

Tapestry: A piece of artwork that is made out of layers of threads and fibers that are woven together on a loom. (39)

Technique: A procedure used to accomplish a specific activity or task. (12, 13, 28, 36, 38)

Three-dimensional: Something that is sculptural: having width, length, and depth. (28)

Two-dimensional: Flat artwork having just width and length. (28)

Woodcut: A type of print made from carving into a piece of wood using different tools. The raised areas left behind are inked and printed. (4, 23, 40)

List of Illustrations

Works that are shown as details in the book are reproduced here in their entirety.

(Front endsheet) *Phil*, **1983**. Pulp paper on canvas, 92 x 72 in. Photograph courtesy The Pace Gallery.

(Page 1) *Judy*, **1989–90**. Oil on canvas, 72 x 60 in. Museum of Modern Art of Fort Worth, TX. Photograph by Bill Jacobson.

(Pages 2 and 31) *Stanley (Large Version)*, **1980–81**. Oil on canvas, 101 x 84 in. Solomon R. Guggenheim Museum, New York, NY. Photograph courtesy The Pace Gallery.

(Page 3) *Lorna*, **1995**. Oil on canvas, 102 x 84 in. The Doris and Donald Fisher Collection at the San Francisco Museum of Modern Art. Photograph by Ellen Page Wilson, courtesy The Pace Gallery.

(Page 5) Photographs of Chuck Close and students © Joel DeGrand. Painting details from *Roy II*, **1994**.

(Page 6) *Mount Rainier*, **c. 1950**. Courtesy of Chuck Close.

(Page 7) *Still Life*, **c. 1950**. Courtesy of Chuck Close. Chuck with pet monkey, 1954. Courtesy of Chuck Close.

(Page 8) *Time* magazine, 1945, cover art by Boris Chaliapin. © 1945 Time, Inc. Reprinted by permission.

(Page 9) Chuck Close drawing caricatures, 1958. Courtesy of Chuck Close.

(Pages 10–11) *Leslie/Water-color*, **1972–73**. Watercolor on paper mounted on canvas, 72½ x 57 in. Photograph by Ellen Page Wilson, courtesy The Pace Gallery.

Alex/Reduction Print, **1993**. Screenprint from reduction carved linoleum, 79⅜ x 60⅜ in., Edition of 35. Photograph by Bill Jacobson.

Lynda, **2004**. Photograph by Kerry Ryan McFate, courtesy The Pace Gallery.

Phil/Fingerprint, **1980**. Stamp-pad ink on paper, sheet: 93 x 69 in. Chase Manhattan Bank Collection, New York, NY. Photograph by Al Mozell, courtesy The Pace Gallery.

(Page 12) Proof sheet for *Big Self-Portrait*, **1967**. Courtesy of Chuck Close.

(Page 13) *Big Self-Portrait* in Close's studio, 1968. Courtesy of Chuck Close.

(Page 14) *Self-Portrait/ 58,424*, **1973**. Ink and pencil on paper mounted on canvas, 70½ x 58 in. Photograph courtesy The Pace Gallery.

(Page 15) *Self-Portrait*, **1986**. Oil on canvas, 54½ x 42¼ in. Photograph by Ellen Page Wilson, courtesy The Pace Gallery.

(Page 16) *Self-Portrait/ Watercolor*, **1976–77**. Water-color on paper mounted on canvas, 80½ x 59 in. Museum Moderner Kunst Stiftung Ludwig, Vienna. Photograph courtesy The Pace Gallery.

(Page 17) *Self-Portrait*, **1987**. Oil on canvas, 72 x 60 in. Photograph by Bill Jacobson.

(Page 18) *Self-Portrait*, **1977**. Hard-ground etching and aquatint, 54 x 41 in. Edition of 35. Walker Art Center, Minneapolis, MN. Photograph by Maggie L. Kundtz, courtesy The Pace Gallery.

(Page 19) *Self-Portrait*, **1999**. Color digital inkjet print, 88 x 68 in. Photograph courtesy The Pace Gallery.

(Page 20) *Self-Portrait Manipulated,* **1982.** Handmade gray paper, air dried, 38½ x 28⅛ in. Edition of 25, No. 29459.30. Photograph by Ellen Page Wilson, courtesy The Pace Gallery.

(Page 21) *Self-Portrait,* **2000–01.** Oil on canvas, 108 x 84 in. The Art Supporting Foundation to the San Francisco Museum of Modern Art. Photograph by Ellen Page Wilson, courtesy The Pace Gallery.

(Page 22) *Self-Portrait,* **1980.** Stamp-pad ink on paper, 15¾ x 11½ in. Photograph by Al Mozell, courtesy The Pace Gallery.

(Page 23) *Self-Portrait,* **2004.** 19-color hand-printed ukiyo-e-woodcut, 28½ x 22¾ in. Edition of 50. Printed and published by Two Palms Press, NY.

(Page 24) *Self-Portrait,* **1995.** Pencil, marker and India ink on paper, 60 x 40½ in. The UBS Art Collection. Photograph by Ellen Page Wilson, courtesy The Pace Gallery.

(Page 25) *Self-Portrait,* **2004–05.** Oil on canvas, 102 x 84 in. Photograph by Kerry Ryan McFate, courtesy The Pace Gallery.

(Page 26) *Self-Portrait/ Pastel,* **1977.** Pastel and ink wash on paper, 30½ x 22 in. Collection Virginia Museum of Fine Arts, Richmond, VA. Photograph courtesy The Pace Gallery.

(Page 27) *Self-Portrait II,* **2009–10.** Oil on canvas, 72 x 60 in. Photograph by Kerry Ryan McFate, courtesy The Pace Gallery.

(Page 28) *Self-Portrait (Maquette),* **2001.** Polaroid photograph mounted on foamcore with ink and tape, 33¼ x 22 in. Photograph by Ellen Page Wilson, courtesy The Pace Gallery.

(Page 29) Chuck Close working on *John,* **1992.** Photograph by Bill Jacobson. *John,* **1992.** Photograph by Bill Jacobson.

(Page 30) *Georgia/Fingerpainting,* **1984.** Photograph courtesy The Pace Gallery.

(Page 32) (Left) *Zhang Huan I (Maquette),* **2008.** (Right) *Zhang Huan II (Maquette),* **2008.** Poloroid photograph mounted on foamcore with ink and tape, each 24 x 20 in. Photograph by G. R. Christmas, courtesy The Pace Gallery. *Zhang Huan I,* **2008.** Photograph by G. R. Christmas, courtesy The Pace Gallery.

(Page 33) *Zhang Huan II,* **2008–09.** Photograph by Kerry Ryan McFate, courtesy The Pace Gallery.

(Page 34) *Fanny/Fingerpainting,* **1985.** National Gallery of Art, Washington, D.C. Photograph by John Back.

(Page 35) *Robert/104,072,* **1973–74.** The Museum of Modern Art, New York. Photograph by Ellen Page Wilson, courtesy The Pace Gallery. Chuck Close at work on *Robert/104,072.* Courtesy of Chuck Close.

(Page 37) *Nancy,* **1968.** Milwaukee Art Museum, Milwaukee, WI. Photograph courtesy The Pace Gallery. *April,* **1990–91.** The Eli and Edythe L. Broad Collection, Los Angeles. Photograph by Ellen Page Wilson, courtesy The Pace Gallery.

(Page 38) *Phil/Watercolor,* **1977.** Photograph by Ellen Page Wilson, courtesy The Pace Gallery. *Phil,* **1980.** Photograph courtesy The Pace Gallery.

(Page 40) (Left) Wood block jigsaw for *Lucas/Woodcut.* (Right) The woodcut in progress. Photographs courtesy Pace Prints.

Lucas/Woodcut, **1993.** Edition of 50. Photograph by Bill Jacobson.

(Page 41) *Self-Portrait,* **1992.** Edition of 70. Photograph courtesy Pace Prints. Chuck Close working on *Self-Portrait,* **1992.** Photograph by John Back. *John,* **1998.** Edition of 80. Photograph courtesy Pace Prints.

(Page 42) *John,* **1998,** State 3. *John,* **1998,** State 5. Photographs courtesy Pace Prints. *Phil II,* **1982.** Edition of 15. Photograph by Maggie L. Kundtz, courtesy The Pace Gallery.

(Page 43) *Phil II,* being made, Dieu Donné Papermill, 1982. *Jud,* **1982.** Virginia Museum of Fine Arts, Richmond, VA. Photograph by Ron Jennings. Chuck Close working on *Jud,* 1982. Photograph by S. K. Yeager, © 1983.

(Page 45) Chuck Close undergoing rehab at Rush Institute with physical therapist Meg Sowarby. Photograph by John Back. Close on "Big Joe" working on *Phyllis/Collage,* 1984. Courtesy of Chuck Close.

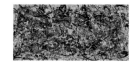

(Page 46) Jackson Pollock, *Number 8, 1949.* Oil, enamel, and aluminum paint on canvas, 34⅛ x 71¼ in. Photograph by Jim Frank. © 2011 The Pollock-Krasner Foundation/Artists Rights Society (ARS) New York. Collection Neuberger Museum of Art, Purchase College, State University of New York, Gift of Roy E. Neuberger. Andy Warhol, *Brillo Soap Pads Box,* **1964,** silkscreen ink on synthetic polymer paint on wood. © 2011 The Andy Warhol Foundation for the Visual Arts, Inc./Artists Rights Society (ARS) New York. Collection of The Andy Warhol Museum, Pittsburgh. Mosaic of Emperor Justinian I at Apse Entry, San Vitale, Ravenna, Italy, (c. 546).

(Page 47) *Self-Portrait,* **2010.** Oil on canvas, 36 x 30 in. Photograph by Kerry Ryan McFate, courtesy The Pace Gallery.

(Pages 48–51) Unless otherwise noted all photographs of the artist and his family courtesy of Chuck Close.

(Page 49) *Betsy Ross Revisited,* c. 1961. Courtesy of Chuck Close.

(Page 50) *John,* **1971–72.** The Eli and Edythe L. Broad Collection, Los Angeles. Photograph by Ellen Page Wilson, courtesy The Pace Gallery. Chuck Close undergoing rehab at Rush Institute with physical therapist Meg Sowarby. Photograph by John Back.

(Page 51) *Alex II,* **1989.** Photograph by Ellen Page Wilson, courtesy The Pace Gallery. *Roy II,* **1994.** Hirshhorn Museum and Sculpture Garden, Smithsonian Institution, Washington, D.C. Photograph by Ellen Page Wilson, courtesy The Pace Gallery. Chuck Close and Robert Storr supervising installation for MoMA retrospective, 1998. © 1998 Tina Barney *President Bill Clinton,* **2006.** Photograph by Kerry Ryan McFate. *Kate,* **2007.** Edition of 10 plus one artist proof. Photograph by Donald Farnsworth, courtesy of Magnolia Editions, Oakland, CA.

(Back endsheet) *Janet,* **1992.** Oil on canvas, 100 x 84 in. Albright-Knox Art Gallery, Buffalo, NY. Photograph by Bill Jacobson.

Library of Congress Cataloging-in-Publication Data

Close, Chuck, 1940–
Chuck Close : face book / by Chuck Close.
    p. cm.
    Includes index.
    ISBN: 978-1-4197-0163-4
    1. Close, Chuck, 1940– —Juvenile literature. 2. Artists—United States—Biography—Juvenile literature. I. Title. II. Title: Face book.
N6537.C54A2 2012
759.13—dc23
[B]   2011034557

Printed and bound in China

10 9 8 7 6 5 4 3 2 1

Abrams Books for Young Readers are available at special discounts when purchased in quantity for premiums and promotions as well as fundraising or educational use. Special editions can also be created to specification. For details, contact specialsales@abramsbooks.com or the address below.

ABRAMS Books
115 West 18th Street
New York, NY 10011
www.abramsbooks.com

© 2012 Glue + Paper Workshop, LLC and Ascha Drake

Chuck Close artwork © Chuck Close, Courtesy Pace Gallery

All other art credits see page 54–55.

A Glue + Paper Workshop Book for Kids created by Joan Sommers and Amanda Freymann, with Ascha Drake.
www.glueandpaper.com

Front cover: (Top) *Self-Portrait*, **1987** (detail). (Middle) *Self-Portrait*, **2000–01** (detail). (Bottom) *Self-Portrait*, **1999** (detail).

Back cover: Photograph of Chuck Close, © Joel DeGrand.

Front endsheet: *Phil,* **1983** (detail).
Page 1: *Judy,* **1990** (detail).
Page 2: *Stanley (Large Version),* **1980–81** (detail).
Page 3: *Lorna,* **1995** (detail).
Back endsheet: *Janet,* **1992** (detail).

ACKNOWLEDGMENTS

This book is based on an interview conducted by twelve 5th grade students from PS 8 in Brooklyn, New York, who visited Chuck Close's studio with their teachers. Thank you to the young artists—Brianna, Kiara, Dennis, Kalen, Brittany, Bey, Gabrielle, Henry, Peter, David, Joel, and Naglis—for your thoughtful questions and insights. And a big thank-you to teaching artist Jenny Bevill and classroom teachers Sarah Green and Julie Shultz, who guided the students in their study of Chuck Close's work.

A huge thank-you to Beth Zopf, studio manager for Chuck Close, who assisted us at every turn.

For providing us with images, we thank Heather Monahan and Eliza Wilson-Powers at The Pace Gallery; Maya Piergies at Pace MacGill; and Austin Kennedy at Pace Prints.

Pat Goley at Professional Graphics came to our rescue, performing his digital magic on several images.

We are grateful to Howard Reeves, our editor at Abrams and a trusted colleague and friend, whose enthusiasm for the book never waned. The team at Abrams—Jenna Pocius, Alison Gervais, and James Armstrong—was wonderful to work with.

Thanks to Joel, Ernie, and Scott for your love and support.

Most importantly, we want to thank Chuck Close for trusting us to help him tell his story to young people. His inspirational autobiography contains a powerful message about the importance of art and art education in all children's lives.

Thank you, Chuck, for your generosity, kindness, and honesty.